JUSTA GUM WRAPPER

BY GINA AND MERCER MAYER

Reader's Digest **Kids**

Westport, Connecticut

My teacher said that we have to take care
of the Earth because it takes care of us.

I didn't know that.

My teacher said
the Earth gives us
a place to live . . .

air to breathe . . .

water to drink . . .

and food to eat.

I guess the Earth really does take care of us.

My teacher said that we also have to take care of the things that the Earth gives us— so that there will be enough for everyone.

I told Mom and Dad. They said
my teacher was smart.
I said, "I want to be careful and
take care of the Earth."
They said that was a good idea.
So we thought of some things
we could do to help.

We try really hard not to throw trash on the ground. One day I had to remind my sister. She said, "It's just a gum wrapper."
I said, "What if everybody in the whole world said that?"
She picked it up.

We turn off the lights when
we're not in the room.
When I'm brave, I even
turn off my night-light.

I still have to remind Dad to turn off the TV when he is sleeping.

DAD! YOU FORGOT TO TURN OFF THE TV!

I never forget to turn off the water
in the tub anymore. Sometimes
I still forget about the sink.

We only buy cleaning stuff that doesn't harm the Earth. And we try to buy things in containers that can be used again.

At home we have special places to put plastic, glass, paper, and cans so that they can be recycled. Recycling is one of the most important things we can do to help.

But sometimes I get mixed up.

Now Mom hangs the wash on the
clothesline instead of using the drier.
I have to be careful not to knock
the clothes down.

We use cloth diapers for my little brother
instead of the kind you throw away. That's
good for the Earth, but it's kind of messy.

A truck comes to bring clean diapers
and take the yucky ones away.

My sister and I try to remember to close
the refrigerator door when we're finished.

Mom's been trying to get us to do that
for a long time.

When we take our empty bottles and cans
to the recycling place, we get money for them.
Mom lets us spend some of the money.
We buy lots of neat stuff.

At school we made a chart to see which family did the most to take care of the Earth in one week. My family won.

There was a class party, and my whole family came. That was fun. I was really proud. I was even proud of my sister.

Then we planted a tree by the playground.
The teacher said it was my special tree for
doing such a good job.

That made Mom and Dad really happy.

I still have a lot to teach my baby brother about taking care of the Earth.